Listen to the Tide

Royale Road Publishing

Listen to the Tide

poems and other musings

Clifton King

Listen to the Tide

Editors: Katie Rose King, Janine Johnson
Cover art: *Night Sky*, by the author

ISBN: 978-0-9786935-5-8

Library of Congress Control Number: 2019914459

Printed in the United States of America

Royale Road Publishing, Carlsbad, California

for my family

If art is to nourish the roots of our culture, society must set the artist free to follow his vision wherever it takes him. We must never forget that art is not a form of propaganda; it is a form of truth. When power leads man towards arrogance, poetry reminds him of his limitations. When power narrows the areas of man's concern, poetry reminds him of the richness and diversity of his existence. When power corrupts, poetry cleanses, for art establishes the basic human truths which must serve as the touchstone of our judgment. John F. Kennedy, at the dedication of the Robert Frost Library, October 26, 1963, Amherst College.

Contents

There is a voice that doesn't use words. Listen.

Rumi

Old Friend

Come in, make yourself comfortable
so we can begin this poem.
I thought I'd start with one of those
November red sunsets, people
gathered in a seaside café staring
out to sea like a flock of seagulls.
And the locals at their favorite spots
along the seawall or strolling
down Carlsbad Boulevard. But, then
we are left with the night, dark and
foreboding along those unlit beaches.
And let's face it, once the sun goes
down they take up the sidewalks
in this part of town. So maybe
we should get up early, take coffee
out to the porch, watch the sun
crawl over the La Costa hills
while it pinks up that morning sky.
Now, we have all day. What would
you like to do old friend? We can
leave this poem unfinished, just
like those dirty dishes in the sink
and that unmade bed.
It will all still be there tomorrow.
But, for us, now is the only certainty.

New Year's Day 2019
a few days after my 75th birthday

Morning air bites at my face. I stuff my hands deep
into my jacket pockets. Beach cobbles rattle
with every attack of waves that rolls ashore.
The sky is pale blue, nearly white along the horizon
where the early sun paints the sea silver.
A few surfers exploit an offering of small swells.
My board lies in wait on the van floor.
I walk water's edge, sand cool, damp beneath bare feet.
The cold granite of the north jetty beckons. I step from
boulder to boulder. A cold ocean surrounds me, gnaws
at the indestructible finger of stone where I stand.
The sea forces herself into crevices and voids
between giant boulders, explodes upward, sea spray
carried on the wind, as cold on my face as this January air.
This is the way to begin a new year. This is the way
it should end someday: the memory of me, the sea
and an ocean breeze. And when the current is right
I'll drift north, join my father when he returns on the tide.

Father

I sat with him for days in the hospital
after his stroke. Too much damage to
the part of his brain that formulates
and deciphers spoken words. Comatose,
he couldn't understand, couldn't express.
I wasn't with my father the night he died.
It's almost as if he never left.
He's somewhere in my life every day:
when I see the ocean, that stretch of sand
where we waded in, set his memory adrift
on the outgoing tide; when I rifle through
his old rusty tool box, find something
he used to build my childhood; when I watch
a sunset, wonder if he found Mother
                                on the other side.

Love Poems

If my poems were strong enough,
each like the stones Jeffers gathered
along the Carmel coast, I would build
a fortress where I could keep the world
at bay, away from our time together.
I could only hope the rain didn't find
those small crevices between my metaphors.
There would be an English garden out back.
I would paint the garden gate green,
if only for the alliteration.
And beyond the garden, the sea, all blustery
with whitecaps, dappled with the same blue
your eyes smile in the afternoon sun.
And from the forest of words that covers
those distant mountains I would harvest
love poems, lay them in the palm of your hand
                              —along with my heart.

Weathervane

A rusty red rooster perched on a rod,
points of the compass suspended below,
sits atop my shed. When I was a boy
it occupied a place of prominence
on the rooftop of Grandpa's barn.
He took morning coffee on the back porch,
studied the weathervane, a bright red then.
Wind is the messenger of God, he would say.
Now, I watch that rusty relic of a vane,
try to decipher its squeaks, that stuttering spin,
wonder if it's a message from Grandpa.

Divine Disclosure

The ocean gives up her bones.
Small shards of shells, the color
of moonlight, litter the shore;
smooth to the touch, weightless
as summer sun in your hand.
I harvest a few wedged among
cobbles still damp from high tide.
The beach is an unmarked canvas
from last night's rain. I shake
pieces of shells in cupped hands,
spill them onto the sand
like a Voodoo bone reader.
Their pattern reveals a secret.
They would speak to a real diviner.
What could they possibly say to me?
Maybe—the reasons I love you.
But, I don't need bits of shells
to tell me what I already know.

After the Storm

I wander out to the porch
the dogs at my feet.
Morning is still part of the night,
its color that same gray
as the belly of young storm clouds.
Coffee steams in my mug.
Its musky blush reminds me
of that woman, her deep cocoa
skin, eyes dark as a starless night.
But, that's another story
for another time. This morning
the ocean, just beyond that row
of expensive homes, beckons.
She brings swells alive with power,
swells that have traveled days
across open ocean to be ridden
before dying on these shores,
swells licked into life by a storm
given a name as if it were a newborn
with a lifetime ahead of it.
I finish my coffee, put the dogs
in the house and venture out
to salvage whatever I can
from the remnants of that storm,
whatever its name was.

Dove Eggs

A mourning dove is nesting
in a hanging plant that sways
with each whisper of sea breeze.
A week ago there were two eggs.
Then the crow that lives in a palm
down the street swooped in, wings
flared, menacing beak agape.
Mother dove flew off in fright.
I grabbed a broom as if I could
sweep away the danger. The crow
laughed as he carried off an egg.
I stood guard for hours, broom
at the ready. Finally, mother dove
returned, a surprised look on her
face when she saw only one egg.
Or is that her usual wide-eyed look?
I check on her daily, not that I can
prevent nature's course. I'm glad
humans don't prey on each other
like animals…………Oh, wait.

Normandy Coast
Omaha Beach

We were there for a week,
unable to speak
for the first few hours,
unable to dry our eyes.
I have a small vile of sand
from Omaha Beach.
I'm not sure why
I collected it,
brought it home.
It was low tide,
the beach
a hundred yards wide.
I was reluctant
to walk on the sand,
like stepping
on someone's grave.
Yet, I had to have
a few grains of that sand,
just as I would cherish
a splinter of the cross
Jesus carried up Calvary.

Addiction

That weekend chaos on Pacific Coast Highway rumbles
passed as I stand at the edge of a bluff above the Pacific.
Below, a thread of beach stretches along the California coast.
It is overrun by the multitudes escaping inland heat.
The vivid reds, blues and greens of beach umbrellas
and sunshades smear the sand with a collage of color
like an impressionist painting. This façade disappears
into that distant haze regurgitated from the LA basin.
The ocean today is lake-like, calm, well mannered,
nearly silent where sea meets sand. The pungent
aroma of rotting, fly infested, seaweed mingles
with the sweet scent of sunscreen and hibachi smoke.
Small children at water's edge scream and laugh
with the pure joy of cold ocean water swirling
around their ankles. Most men and women on the beach
are attired in swimwear they really should reconsider.
But, I'm not here to judge. I'm here for my ocean fix.
I take a hit of sea breeze, drop a little summer sky,
mainline this late June sun and that lazy line of pelicans.

Beyond Retrieval

How quickly the axe fell, the thick thud
of my head into a basket. Only moments
before I was a Prince, my words
and Shakespeare's uttered in the same breath,
words that could win a woman's heart.

Then —
the transformation, that transgression,
as if by magic, Prince to village idiot.

But there was no magic, no evil spell
cast by witch or warlock. Only the stupidity,
the insensitivity that men have nurtured
since the beginning: speak first, think later.

The axe fell, insuring no repeat offense.
Words spoken cannot be retrieved.

Across Baja and Back
Circa 1972 riding a BSA 500cc single

Yesterday the road from Ensenada to San Felipe was nothing more
than a dry, meandering scar across the Baja peninsula: one-hundred-
sixty miles of sand, rocks, dry riverbeds and more rocks. We raised
a dust cloud that didn't settle until nightfall. This morning, rain
ricochets off the Sea of Cortez, murky water washes cobble-strewn
beaches. The musty odor of wet earth hangs heavy in the air. This is
a desert ride. Rain was never a consideration. We eat breakfast in a
small cantina packed with locals. There is a plate of warm tortillas
that never runs out, like a Denny's all-you-can-eat pancake
breakfast. A din of rapid fire Spanish fills the room. A blue haze of
cigarette smoke lingers in the air. Unable to postpone our departure
any longer we head west toward the Pacific and Highway One.
Rain pelts our helmets and goggles, stings our faces. When we
reach the edge of Diablo Dry Lake the rain stops. The sky begins to
clear. Baja resembles a moonscape: ragged ravines, plateaus, that
faint purple of distant mountains. Valle De La Trinidad and the little
town of Colonia Cardenas lie beyond the Sierra De Juarez
Mountains. With our non-existent Spanish we ask an old man if
there is someplace to get food. He turns, wanders off without saying
a word. We follow him to the local bar, a brick building with no
glass in the windows, no door in the doorway. Inside, there is more
shadow than light. The beer is cool, not cold. We eat tortillas filled
with a cheese-like substance, leafy greens, possibly lettuce, and a
killer salsa made from jalapenos and nitroglycerin. Next stop
Ensenada. Once home, it takes two days for the numbness to leave
your back side, a week before your sinuses are free of Baja dust.
And never again will you believe that anything from Taco Bell
is really Mexican food.

Duck Bread

My six-year-old granddaughter arrives
already in her SpongeBob SquarePants PJs,
hair damp from her after school bath.

Then, a ritual practiced by all grandchildren:
she goes through my pockets for loose change.
But she finds my money clip, takes the bills,
stashes them in a zip-lock bag on the bookshelf
next to her mermaid Barbie Doll.

Now, the most important decision of the day:
blow bubbles on the front porch, play golf
on the putting green or feed the ducks.

Do you have any duck bread, she asks.
I produce a bag of freshly diced bread
purchased off the day-old rack at Ralph's.

She runs to her bedroom, returns with a pair
of those rubber shoes you buy at Walmart.
It doesn't matter that they're two sizes too big,
because, they are pink, adorned with a princess.

I hold her hand as we shuffle down the street,
her resplendent in yellow and pink. And I know
I'm about to get another chance at a moment
in time when a bag of duck bread
          is the most important thing in life.

Limits

Our limits are often set by others:
our speed rolling down PCH,
the number of checks you can write
without a service charge, the amount
of data available on your phone plan.
Some limits we place on ourselves when
common sense overrides testosterone:
admit when the surf is too gnarly,
a white shark sighting too recent.
So, we stay in our favorite beach chair,
listen to the constant music
of the Pacific Ocean, question why
seagulls gather on the sand,
always face into the wind
like a flock of weathervanes.

Half Mast

Old Glory flies at half mast.
Not a whisper of wind.
Like a head hung low
in heartbreaking sorrow,
stars and stripes drape lifeless
against the flagpole.
This display of grief and respect
is for a former President.
Yet, it's become too common
a sight: flags flying at half mast
for students massacred
in their classrooms,
for innocent people
slaughtered in God's house,
for celebrators murdered
in theaters and nightclubs.
Flags, soaked in tears,
fly at half mast. Yet,
our outrage is ignored,
hollow condolences
handed out like campaign promises.

At Our Beach

I sit with sun on my face,
realize the glow I feel
comes from my thoughts of you.

I wonder how long
I've given the sun credit
for the warmth of our love?

Alone

Years after my mother's death,
Father still lives in their home.

He tells me, *There are too many*
memories in this place.
Not a day goes by I don't talk to her.
At night, I reach across the bed
—before I remember.

Father lives alone, yet he still
sleeps only on his side of the bed.

Wind-Bells and Children

Our wind-bell hangs from a porch beam, prompted
into song by ocean breezes, storm whipped winds
and on occasion it seems to sing out on its own.
It was an anniversary gift from our son's then girlfriend.
She is now, like yesterday's wind-bell song, in the wind.
This bronze bell is one-of-a-kind, born of fire, hammer
and anvil in Cosanti's foundry. Each bell a descendent
of Paolo Soleri's vision. The bell's unique tone reminds
me of my children; lives gone different directions, forged
by the same hand and vision, sent out into the world
to find their place, sing their song.

*Cosanti, located in Paradise Valley, Arizona, is the headquarters, foundry, studio,
and gallery for Paolo Soleri bronze & ceramic wind-bells & sculptures.

7.8 Quake, Nepal

Twenty-one dead on Everest.
Nine thousand more
in the villages of Nepal.
One million children
in need of humanitarian aid.
The climbers knew the risk,
accepted the odds of never returning.
The others, mothers with infants
strapped to their backs, men at work
waiting to see families at the end of the day,
children in schools at play,
unaware of the risks of everyday life.
We all believe the odds are in our favor.

A Drive up Pacific Coast Highway

Palatial balconies jut from multi-million-dollar homes.
Vacant patio chairs, gas grills hidden beneath dusty
covers stand silent as barbeque utensils rust in ocean air.
But I don't see a single person. I never do. So, where are
the people who first stepped onto their deck,
saw the sparkle of sun on the Pacific, heard the ocean's
voice welcome them to the neighborhood? Did they stay
long enough to see the spectacle of November's red sunsets;
listen to the laugh of gulls; feel those wisps of morning fog
creep ashore; watch an informal formation of pelicans
stitch clouds to the sky? Or was it always about resale value?
What a shame, blinded by a few coins of the realm.

Twenty-two

shot dead while shopping
in a Walmart in Texas, 8/4/19

Twenty-two people,
fellow human beings
from south of the border,
here for a day—dead.
A horrific act prompted
by the color
of someone's skin,
by the rhetoric of a moron
in the highest office,
rooted in evil that believes
white to be supreme.
(I wouldn't print the name
of the monster responsible
if my life depended on it.)
How can any person harbor
that much hate?
How can this happen
again and again: shoppers,
students, church goers?
Politicians refuse to act,
turn away in cowardice.
Families cry.
But, tears can't stop the bullets.

You might quiet the whole world for a second if you pray.
And if you love, if you really love, our guns will wilt.

St. John of the Cross

Blue Dress

You're wearing
that blue dress
the universe
insisted on;
I'm wondering
what I ever did
to deserve
a woman like you;
and outside
the window
pelicans drift by,
stare at
our wedding guests.

Watching Sunset from the Porch
during the California wildfires of 2018

A dog barks in the distance.
The blather of Fox News on
our neighbor's TV muscles its way
into our solitude. On the street
a motorcycle thunders past.
Its staccato song stirs yearnings
for my youth, for those miles
of adolescent highways swallowed
by two wheels, the straight pipe rasp
of a parallel twin. Our wind-bell
is silent. Yet, fronds of our palm
rustle in a late Santa Ana wind.
The muted mix of waves washing
across cobbles, the dull whisper
of the evening commute hang
in the air. This evening's sunset
is a blood red display, smoke
from wildfires up north, the ghost
of everything it took lifetimes to build.

Before I Leave

It's hard to imagine becoming complacent
about our love: being too used to you
to not open a door; not offer to carry in
groceries; not whisper a goodnight, *I love you.*
I know the evening sun always kisses
the horizon before vanishing into the night
and an ocean wave's last act is to caress
the rock and sand of a willing coastline.
So my love, on that day I die,
I pray I can open the door one final time,
make sure you are safe inside before I leave.

Thornton Hospital

lobby
security station
check-in
gift shop
cafeteria
powder rooms
people of every color
wheelchairs
walkers
canes
limps
potted palms
scrubs
white coats
slow walkers
shufflers
young men
old men
old women
young women
three hours
your Doctor
his smile
I can breathe again

Between Sun and Water
after the art of Sherry Krulle Beaton
—*Between Sun and Water*

It stands on a bluff above the Pacific,
gnarled from decades of coastal winds,
bare branches skeletal against
a sun-drenched sky, not a single leaf
to give hope for greener days.
When I was a child, concerned only
with wading in the blue Pacific,
sand castles and how high I could fly
my kite, this tree was alive with promise.
Now, having grown old together,
this tree and I can only stand between
sun and water, wait for that final sunset.

The Truth on Valentine's Day

I may have written this poem before.
Yet, my intent is not to gift you
second-hand words. I can only
speak of love in present tense.
These words are no less heartfelt
just because I may have scribbled
them in an earlier poem. I did
search for a new combination
of letters to express my love
for you. But, you see I've already
fallen into the conventional
with my use of *love*. There are
a plethora of words which express
this same thought, none acceptable.
So, the letters I have chosen are:
                    You are my life.

Patio Bench

It's a blue nearly as dark
as a night sky, with a hint
of purple. You can find
it on most Mexican pottery,
this night blue, this almost
purple. Our patio table
has tiles this color. Flowers
and birds wend their way
across this dark background.
I want the bench that color,
she says. So I cut and miter,
sand and paint until I have
twenty odd pieces of wood
that should come together
as a patio bench. And they do.
Now, when we sit in the sun
on our new blue patio bench
we are reminded of my plan
to build it, her desire
for a certain color and
our partnership that made
it possible, like everything
                    in our lives.

Truths

No matter the questions,
these are not answers,
nor the pretense, just truths
that hold minutes together.

The click of a doorknob
when it's turned;
blades of grass
that stick to your shoes
on a dewy morning;
train whistles at night,
crying through empty crossings.

Father's Two-Bubble Level

The other fathers on our block played golf on the weekend.
My father sawed and sanded wood. He mitered, nailed,
and glued with abandon. It was the 1950s. Each month
Popular Mechanics published plans for a woodworking project.
My father ripped those plans from the magazine, laid them
on his workbench. On Sunday my father and I would visit
the lumber yard in Bellflower. My sisters stayed home with
Mother. This was men's work, finding just the right boards
for this month's project. Over the years Father built tables
and chairs, bedroom furniture and patio benches.
Then, he built a small room in the corner of our garage.
It was the first time I ever saw a bubble level. Today, that level
hangs in my shed, the only tool of my father's I still have.
Its mahogany body scratched and faded; the brass, lackluster.
But both horizontal and vertical glass tubes still hold a bubble
after nearly seventy years. And at one end the maker's mark
barely readable: The Peerless Level & Tool Company,
Sterling, Ill. Every time I hold it in my hand, wait for that bubble
to settle, reveal the accuracy of my work, I think of Father.
He was a kind man. He was my hero. The worst I ever heard
him say of another human was, *He's about half a bubble off.*

Love Gifts

I bring my love cobbles from the beach, for her garden.
I choose them with care, look for something unusual.
Though in truth they are all unique, as different
from one another as you and I. But, even with their
on-of-a-kind uniqueness, they are nearly worthless
on the open market. True, they might be used to build
a cobblestone street like those narrow pathways
in every European village; those Colonial carriageways
beneath the cracked asphalt roads of Philadelphia.
So, I carry them home, rough and still dusty
with beach sand, place them in her hand, remind her
that these rocks have memorized the summer sun's
warmth; their shape smoothed by eons of tumbling
in tides. Yet, they cannot be quantified in carats,
like precious stones, because love is immeasurable.

The Ugly Americans
—apologies to Burdick & Lederer

They've committed no crimes,
these children of illegal immigrants.
Yet, let's punish them anyway.
This is America.
It's a matter of national security.
These frightened five-year-olds
pose an indisputable threat.
Show them how tough
tRump can be on the defenseless.
This is America.
Take a page from Joe Arpaio's book.
Cowardly truck them out at night
to somewhere in the wilds of Texas,
a tent city in the desert, a prison
by any name. Don't tell a soul
where you've taken them.
That would make it too easy
for their lawyers, their parents.
But don't worry about it,
the Republicans don't and they
know what is best for America.
Vote Democrat—or die.

Warm Water Jetty 2019

The wind is out of the north, gusting cold.
I wander the bluff above the sea at Terra Mar.
There is a waning swell from last week's storm.
A few surfers bob randomly in the ocean,
stare at the horizon. But the super tide pushes
every wave to shore before allowing it to break.
I work my way down to the beach where
Warm Water Jetty used to jut into the surf
just south of the power plant outflow.
Now, only a skeleton of boulders remains.
I find one that provides a protected perch,
its surface rough and warm. This black basalt
boulder has memorized the afternoon sun.
The sea forces its way up a cobbled slope,
turns, rushes back into itself. The ocean roars
with the frenzy of pebbles dragged out to sea.
I sit alone in this place awash in memories.
It was 1963 when I first came to this beach.
Jimmy and I drove down from Lakewood,
two balsa boards tied to the roof of his Vee Dub.
We parked along the bluff, long before a seawall
and the parking lot at Tamarack. Twenty six
years later I returned and called it home.
This is the beach where I met Jeff and Rob
one Saturday morning in '93. This beach
where, for decades, we shared friendship,
the waves and our love for the ocean.
Jeff is gone now. He used up those twelve
extra years his heart-transplant bought him.
Rob moved to Oregon a decade ago. For years
I've come to sit on the jetty, listen to the waves.
Now, the jetty is gone, like many friends
and a few family. But listen, do you hear that?
The sea still has stories to tell.

Running Shoes

I wear running shoes:
bright blue with silver accents,
soles made of some secret
compound developed by NASA
for our Astronauts. But,
I'm almost certain Astronauts
don't run around in the space station
or while orbiting Earth in the shuttle.
I don't run either: old knees; a body
tossed to the ground too many times
by my motorcycle in a desert race
or on a mountain trail when I was young
and immortal. Oh, I jogged for health,
fitness and once in a half-marathon
during those years between youth
and….maturity. I wear running shoes
every day for that bounce they put
in my step, for that psychological
connection to my stronger years.
This morning I walk the beach
in search of driftwood, but instead
find a quagmire of black stinking tar.
My running shoes don't understand
the danger, don't recognize the threat.
They are now in a box in the shed.
I fear the bounce in my step, my ardor
for life might diminish without them.
Then, I see you on the porch, afternoon
sunlight on your face. *How was your walk?*
The music of your voice reminds me
that you are the bounce in my step.

Shells

Seashells from the beaches of Mexico.
Small, conical, now empty of any life,
once home to Sea of Cortez creatures.

My mother's only possessions
I can still hold in my hand, touch
like she touched, feel like she felt.

They lie on my bookshelf alongside
the poetry books. I count fourteen,
not that the number is important.

Most are ocher with white swirls,
yet no two are identical. They could
be the fingerprints of the sea.

One shell is distinctly different, more
beautiful. It conjures up memories
of the last time I saw my mother.

Ponto Beach
second day of 2019

A January breeze persuades me to slip on a sweatshirt.
The sea sparkles with sunlight. Wispy lines of whitewater
streak its surface. A couple walks at water's edge, barefoot,
pants rolled up. The cold ocean swirls around their ankles.
A small child scurries down the beach, tries to tease
her kite into flight. A dog runs loose on the sand. Seagulls
sit atop wooden poles that hold up volleyball nets.
I stuff my hands deep into my sweatshirt pockets. The sky
is a cloudless slate blue that morphs to silver white
at that razor sharp line where sea and sky meet. Meager
morning surf beckons half a dozen surfers. With every surge
of sea, the rattle of cobbles. I step up onto the north jetty:
granite chunks the size of a child's bed, blasted from
some distant mountain; laid with such precision, top so flat
you can walk as easily as strolling down Coast Highway.
At jetty's end I sit, face south so the wind is at my back,
sun on my face. Near me an old man fishes in the channel
between the jetties. My father was a fisherman. He told
stories of my mother and him fishing the Sea of Cortez, their
small aluminum boat, that stray cat they fed while cleaning fish,
their rusty water tank, those decades they had together.
                              Now, they have eternity.

When I began to listen to poetry, it's when I began to listen to the stones, and I began to listen to what the clouds had to say, and I began to listen to others.

Joy Harjo

Imagine
— for Katie Rose

Imagine rain that never falls,
trees that never wear leaves,
a garden where no roses grow,

a sea with not a single wave.
Imagine the sky without blue.

That is me without you.

Last Photo of My Parents

The photo is a close-up.
Maybe what they call a *head shot*
in the world of celebrities and models.
Father has a full beard, a red bandana
around his neck, a wide brimmed straw hat
on his head. Mother is wearing a pink
Hello Kitty top, a blue bandana
and floppy white hat to guard against
the unrelenting Mexican sun.
I'm not sure who took the snapshot.
Probably a stranger they just met.
The background suggests a palapa,
perhaps somewhere on the Sea of Cortez.
My father's eyes are that startling blue,
my mother's smile certainly no harbinger
of what claims her mere months later.

Then She Wept

In early February of this year, a young couple
was married on a Sunday. The next day
John Thomas Hill left for work on his motorcycle.
He died moments later.

John Thomas Hill, you left so soon.
Your future sits alone,
huddled within herself, asking why,
knowing there is no answer,
none that she will ever hear.

You rode into the early mist,
like a knight with sword and armor,
your steed racing toward battle.
Death was never a thought.
Death is for the old and the weak.

John Thomas, you were neither.
How then, did your life become
scattered across the battlefield?

A brave mount stumbles,
your shield lowered.
Inexperience and indecision
are swift enemies.
The slash of a blade,
armor pierced,
crushed beneath your foe.

Final words uttered,
heard only by God.

Poolside Umbrella

It's a red that would embarrass
a late November sunset.
Blood red might be a good
description. But, I'm afraid
that color reflected on the pool's
surface might attract sharks.
And behind the red umbrella,
in the old brick planter,
a bird of paradise blooms, shaded,
this time of day, by five tall palms.
A hummingbird busies herself
in the shadows. A few feet
from me a dragonfly dips
for a drink, then shoots off to
......I'm not sure where.
A monarch butterfly flits franticly
from fern to fern in search
of a place to lay her eggs, wondering,
I'm sure, *Where are the milkweed?*
Beyond the palms another red
catches my eye: the seven red
stripes on Old Glory, her colors
vivid against the afternoon sky.
An ocean breeze ruffles her stripes
and I swear I hear someone singing
                    America The Beautiful.

The Sea

The sea
is my woman,
my lover.
This morning
she has little
to offer,
other than
just being there
for me.
Yet, I manage
to embrace
the face
of a few waves
she surrenders.

Not a Sonnet

As a poet I've written a sonnet or two,
struggled with reasonable rhymes,
if there is such a thing; counted
syllables; worried about meter;
hoped I could say it all in the allotted
fourteen lines. Generally, I was
more concerned about form than words.
That's not poetry. That's a math problem;
that's building a brick wall, carful
the spacing is exact; that's a recipe
for chicken so you don't feed the family
something inedible for dinner.

Tower 22 at Ponto Beach
inspired by the art of Kim Hirch-*Blue Tower*

This morning's sky is still a part of the night,
bluer than that lifeguard tower, bluer than
the eyes of a woman I loved in my youth.
Walk with me into this art, feel the sand
damp underfoot, unmarked, smooth
from last night's rain; come with me
to water's edge where the beach
gives way to a long scar of cobbles;
listen to the voice of the ocean, a chaotic
concert of breaking waves; breathe air
baptized in salt water; gather sunlight,
put it in your pocket along with any
shells we might find. And look, beyond
that spindly legged tower, beyond
those eroding coastal bluffs, a faint dab
of white: the Encinas power plant,
smokestack spewing steam.
But what I really want to do while
we are here is climb the blue tower's
ramp, lie on its deck and beg the sun
to give us a sky this blue again tomorrow.

Locked Door

Some days
there is a door,
a room,
a sanctuary
where we can
re-learn secrets
long forgotten;
find that child
who first
frolicked
in a sea-wash
of waves; who
chased seagulls
down long
sloping sands;
marveled at
black birds,
egrets and eagles,
those wind wisps
that carry them
like spring pollens.
Yet, some days
that door
to yesterday
is difficult to open.

Oath
following the El Paso shooting

Lights blaze atop police cars.
Miles of crime scene tape
flutters in the aftermath.
Like cattle at a watering hole
ambulances gather,
wait to swallow up wounded.
Veronica Escobar re-states
the El Paso people's position:
This man, No.45, is not welcome.

No.45 is salt in the open wound
American democracy has become,
his rhetoric the festering sores
of bigotry, racism and hatred.
It's impossible to accept
that nothing is being done,
horrifying to know
this will not be the last time.
I swear I will never speak
this man's name again—ever.

Old Dogs

There are dogs in my house, in my life.
I want to write a poem about them,
maybe mention unconditional love,
how they curl up next to me
on the couch, content with any
TV program I choose to watch;
get excited about taking a walk;
jump on the bed when I lie down;
lick my face just because I'm there;
protect me from UPS & FedEx trucks.
But, I remember a poem written
by the late Jimmy Stewart, how
he read it on the Johnny Carson show,
a posthumous tribute for his dog Beau.
His poem rhymed with some predictable
lines. But, he read it with his signature
soft stammer, decades of acting
experience, a slight catch in his voice
and moist eyes. So I ask you
—what chance do I have?

I Can't Write That Poem

I haven't written anything yet
about our night together.
Meaningful moments are the most
difficult to translate into words.
Everything I tried sounded cliché.
Unlike a poem about the sea,
desert dunes or crisp mountain air,
love demands more on the page.
So my love, until I can invent
words that look as good on paper
as you feel in my arms,
          I can't write that poem.

Becoming a Poet

During those days in the shadow
of my divorce, after my high school
sweetheart and I went different
directions, I turned to poetry
to occupy my mind, fill that void
of togetherness and the warmth
of human touch. I consumed poetry
books like manna from Heaven.
I read the *how to* books written
by prominent poets. I attended
workshop after workshop, ruined
one notebook after another
with bad verse, phrases I could not
marry into a poem. Months
and years passed and I became
a slightly less incompetent poet.
Then one night at Magee Park,
in the old Twin Inns Granary,
I stood before a small gathering
and offered up my words.
I was nervous. They were polite.
From that evening on I called
myself *Poet*. Now, I struggle daily
to bring honor to my new name.

I Don't Miss You Anymore

Those first few weeks I awoke
every night to the fright
of not knowing, not wanting
to be alone. I left the lights on.
The radio played day and night.
Dread was a truckload of bricks
on my chest. I couldn't catch
my breath for a month.
It's been a decade and a half.
I've watched our granddaughter
grow into a young lady,
listened to our son cry
when he lost his son,
and met a woman I want
to be with forever.
I don't miss you anymore.
So, why did I write this poem?

Sunday Afternoon

I spend the morning drinking coffee,
wondering what I might fix for dinner.
At the moment this is all that seems important.

I have yet to glimpse your eyes, questioning
from the shadow of your sun hat.

I have yet to struggle for breath
when you look my way and smile.

I have yet to feel desire wash over
me, uncontrollable as a rogue wave.

So I spend this morning unaware
of the glorious gift God will send
my way this Sunday afternoon.

A Morning at Beacon's

The steel guard rail along the bluff
at Beacon's leans toward the sea
a hundred feet below. The earth
is eroding, falling apart, not unlike
today's society, the political system,
justice system, the very fibers
of the American fabric.
There are signs on the guardrail
that warn of a failing bluff, danger.
Again, not so different than
those signs we see every day:
a warning of incompetence,
rambling rants, evidence of ignorance.
I take the trail down to the beach:
a switchback scar on the face
of the bluff, a few wooden steps
here and there. Low tide pushes the sea
back into itself, births a vast expanse
of sand warm from a morning sun.
I walk water's edge, each surge of sea
erases my footsteps, any evidence
I was ever here. Mother Earth struggles
to heal herself. We ignore her cries.

Looking for Inspiration

My muse has abandoned me, much like my first wife.
The page lies blank in front of me. It doesn't matter
how many deep breaths I take, how many times
I crack my knuckles, how long I stare—it's not there.
I grab a few poetry books from the shelf, head off
to the pool looking for some inspiration. I find
a chair against the wall, away from the crowd.
There are more old bodies here than in a cemetery.
My iPod plugged into my brain, I search through
the poetry books, hope for something I can steal,
something that will get me started. Then, David
shows up, sits beside me. *How's our resident poet?*
I tell him I'm someplace else—try to convey my
desire not to visit. He doesn't catch on. We discuss
overthrowing the management company, touch
on a plan to secede from the union and of course
get deep into our right not to pay federal income tax.
David stands suddenly, mutters something about
colored lights and voices, and abruptly walks away.
I continue my search for something to write about.

Fish Head

It lies on the carpet of pebbles
a few feet from water's edge,
eye sockets vacant. That thin
layer of scales that once covered
the head, gone, picked clean
by seagulls. Its jaw is clenched
in a grim scowl, small razor-like
teeth exposed, a short section
of backbone with its spiny vertebrae
is still attached. This morning's
high tide may have washed it
ashore, the victim of a hungry seal,
or the discard of a fisherman.
I pick it up, take a few steps
toward the water, toss it
into the sea, back to its beginning.
That is where I want to end,
spend eternity riding the tides.

Poetry is a way of taking life by the throat.

Robert Frost

Pig Slop

We all know his name.
But, I refuse to say it,
refuse to ruin this page
with those five, bigoted,
moronic, racist letters.
They are the only things
that really matter to him,
which is ironic since he
has no use for the alphabet,
has never once uttered
an intelligible phrase.
But, say his name
and he perks up like a hog
at the sight of the slop bucket.

We've Let Our Children Down

Childhood should be
a time of happiness
not a time to die
from a burst of bullets,
not a time to die
by the hands of a classmate,
not a time to die
because the NRA
has tRump
in their pocket,
not a time to die
because Washington
is more concerned
about contributions
and reelection
than our children's lives,
not a time to die
because we don't shout
loud enough,
not a time to die
because too few
of us exercise
our right to vote,
not a time to die
because so many
have become
so complacent.

First Kiss

Remember
that sliver of moon
that shone
over my shoulder
the first time
we kissed;
how I pressed
myself against
your willing body?
And is it just me,
or did the stars
explode
when our lips met?

Where I Grew Up

That Southern California neighborhood where I grew up is gone.
Not the actual small wood framed houses squatting, street after
street, on postage stamp sized lots, single car garages, miles of
sidewalks straight as railroad tracks stretched across the Mojave.
But, my sisters are not there now, with their irritating girl friends,
or T.J. Harrison who let me drive his Chevy coupe before I even
had my learner's permit, or his little brother Bobby, or Tommy
Emerson, that fat kid down the block who always wanted to fight,
or the Spencer boy whose father was a Doctor and all the parents
wondered why they lived in our neighborhood, or Curt and Stevie
who stayed with their grandparents next door every summer and
came over to watch Saturday morning cowboy shows on our black
and white TV, and gone are those bicycle rides to Signal Hill and
building forts in the dairy pasture, and Jimmy Davis and his sister
Julie who found their father hanged in the garage one day after
school, and Charlie across the street who congratulated me on my
twelfth birthday saying, *Now you're a teenager*, and gone are those
summer night games of hide 'n seek, and Roy the ice cream man,
swiping pomegranates from old man Slater's backyard, and Cindy
who liked to make out in the back seat after a school dance.
Those were the times I treasure, before the world tried to make us
get in line, march to their music, fight their war, die for their cause.

Old Man Sitting on the Seawall

inspired by the art of Kevin Daly-*The Old Waterman*

She ran off with another man.
Not that I can really blame her,
all those years I spent chasing waves
in Costa Rica, Hawaii and Mexico,
never home long enough to see
she was drifting away, that I was
losing the only woman I ever loved.
That's not true of course. The sea
has always been my first love.
You see those waves behind me,
perfectly shaped, as if an artist
painted them. That's what I lived
for, that was the shape that drove
me insane the way the curve
of a woman's leg, the line
of her neck or small of her back
can push a man over the edge.
But my time is over.
I had decades of that love affair,
caressed by the sea, summer sun
whispering life's secrets. But I heard
only what I wanted and refused
to see the truth. Now, I have only
my memories and this wall where
I sit and watch as my lover embraces
the young man I once was.

The Same Blue as Your Eyes

I'm drowning
in images of the sea,
waves struggle
against shore,
the sun sets
behind a mock landscape
of clouds.
And in that silent slant
of November sky
I glimpse the same blue
as your eyes.

A Small Piece of Time

A chip of concrete, not much bigger
than the end of my thumb, lies on my desk.
It could have come from a broken sidewalk,
the foundation of an old building or maybe
even a school yard basketball court.
It's as white as a December moon. There
is a dark chunk of aggregate in one end,
a miniscule slice of some far-off mountain
quarried by unidentifiable men in a year
that is impossible to guess. But I do know,
one day, a few years back, San Francisco fog
crept under The Golden Gate Bridge, over
the chilly waters of The Bay toward Alcatraz.
The Bridge faded from sight, became merely
an orange aberration dancing above the wake
of our boat. We reached The Rock just as mist
swallowed the afternoon sun. We visited
the cellblocks, held the cold steel of prison bars
in our hands and wandered the exercise yard
where men guilty of unspeakable crimes
were allowed to mingle, smoke cigarettes
and be reminded of those tall concrete walls.
This chip is a flake from that wall. I hold it
between my fingertips. It is rough, it is cold,
just like the men it held captive.

Seashells

I walk water's edge,
wet sand cool beneath bare feet.
In the distance,
the rumble of Coast Highway.
But, the song of the sea, waves
breaking on shore, comforts me.
I scan the sand for unbroken shells,
a gift to give my love.
When I was a child, wandering
the shores of Seal Beach,
high tide would often carpet
the sand with perfect seashells.
There were as many shells as stars,
as many shells as days in a lifetime.
Today, I find only one unbroken shell.

A Short History of My Life

It's all there to see, just lying around, scattered over the landscape
of the last 75 years. Infancy, thrust upon me at an early age, no
regard for my own wishes. All I wanted was to be a cowboy.
But diapers and curly blond locks defined my life in the beginning.
There was the military academy. A decade of khaki uniforms and
spit-shined shoes. Public school was a shock. There were girls: girls
who traveled in packs, girls who'd make out in the hall if you asked,
girls you couldn't even talk to. There were Luckies and Pall Malls
rolled in tee-shirt sleeves, levis we never washed, white bucks and
enough butch wax to choke the proverbial horse. We were *bitchin'*.
College—what can I say, I went surfing. I married young. There
was a family, and years that just slipped away. My children took
their own paths, so did my wife. Retirement looked good, so I did.
I found a new woman, or maybe she found me. Who the hell knows
how those things work. Now, I'm wondering about tomorrow,
not promised to anyone. So, in the morning we'll all find out
together—end of story, or one more page in our history book.

Finding an *I Love You*

I toss an *I love you* into the sea,
hope it returns on the changing tide.
The sun slips silently below the horizon
to become someone else's sunrise.
Our sky darkens to the purple of night.
Stars fall on the ocean. Their fire floats
next to a pale sliver of new moon,
neither as bright as your eyes. I find
yesterday's *I love you* washed ashore,
tangled in the tail of a shooting star.
Unable to separate them I bring both
home, a gift to go with all those others:
the unbroken shells, rocks that shimmer
when wet but become pallid as they dry,
pieces of driftwood, chunks of fallen trees,
bits of bamboo and every *I love you*
I ever offered up in your name.

In the Moment

We can't find the words.
But then, we don't really
want to talk about it.

So, the questions go unasked,
unanswered and we find what
we want in each other.

This is the way lovers live:
in the moment, whispering
promises in present tense.

Discreet Disposal

They don't allow you to keep your loved ones
once the heart has stopped. You can't take them home,
bury them in the backyard like your poodle.
They won't let you wrap them in a burial cloth,
place them in a cave like Jesus. You can't load them
onto a raft, push them out to sea, ablaze in the night,
like some old Viking warrior. They won't allow
a taxidermist to prepare them to sit in a wicker chair
on the patio. And don't even think about stuffing them
with spices and precious oils like the Egyptian Pharos
so they can spend the afterlife in an old trunk in the garage.
I'm not sure it's fair that at the end strangers dress us,
comb our hair, make sure we have a smile, even though
we certainly couldn't be happy about our situation.
I don't want to be on display so people can come, view,
then have free food and lie about what a great guy I was.
I don't want to hear that lid being nailed on, feel the sway
as I'm lowered into the ground where worms and bugs wait.
I'd rather be slipped over the side of a ship, food for the fishes,
maybe even a shark. But these musings are moot. I have years.
Though, it is true, I'm not privy to God's plans.

Seven
for Katie Rose
on our seventh wedding anniversary

Somewhere in my past, while talking
with someone I believed to be a wise person,
I was told that wood was the traditional
seventh anniversary theme gift. So,
I planned for this day, made a trip up north,
purchased the entire California redwood forest.
I had plans to clear cut, have every board foot
delivered to our door. There I would slice,
saw and shave, create windmills, birdbaths
and maybe your favorite….a fleet of frogs.
All this to show the depth, the very fiber
of my love. Of course, the environmentalists
stepped in, hugged the trees and filed suit.
Then, while searching Google for a lawyer,
I discovered a conflicting statement
about that seven year gift thing. It seems
copper and wool are the traditional gifts.
But baby, tradition aside, I still want
           to give you some wood.

Down PCH on a '59 Triumph

My hobby, or what I do in my spare time,
is motorcycle. *James Dean*

I'm seventeen years old.
The rasp of a British twin fills the air.
The highway is fog-bound, my tee-shirt
plastered to my chest, rivulets of moisture
crawl across the lenses of my sunglasses.
That youthful certainty of immortality
won't allow me to wear a helmet.
Wind ties my long, sun bleached hair
into knots as the mechanical beast
beneath me eats asphalt at an alarming rate.
The cacophony of howling tires,
valve clatter, slap of primary chain
and of course that desperate scream
of an engine with straight pipes
takes me to a high second only
to the raw, fear awakening acceleration.
And that girl on the back, arms wrapped
tightly around me, shouts, *I love you.*
But I know it's the adrenaline of speed,
that unspoken presence of danger talking.
I know it's the motorcycle.
And that's okay with me.

Wednesday, June 5, 2019

Our entire life is comprised
of eight years, two months,
twelve days and a smattering
of hours, every minute
of which I have memorized.
That way, when I find myself
alone, for whatever reason,
I can call up a time of pleasure,
of laughter, a time of passion.
But, my love, it is such
a difficult decision with
so many wonderful times
from which to choose.

UCLB 1961

Sue is a surfer from Ventura
with straw colored hair, a smile that
raises my blood pressure. Her eyes,
the color of that seldom seen
green flash, dance when she speaks.
Flawless skin glows a deep tan,
like coffee with too much cream.
A slight smear of pink lipstick
adorns her mouth. We meet most
mornings in the college parking lot;
our token effort at attending classes.
More days than not, we choose now
over the future. My old Chevy
spews blue smoke as we head
for Seal Beach, five miles down PCH.
The campus, perched on a green hillside
with its web of walkways, its halls
of learning, fades in the rear view mirror,
along with our collegiate career.

Youth

The girl was a beautiful brunette,
eyes dark as a starless night.
It was a summer evening drive down
Highway 41, San Luis Obispo County.
Wind swirled around us, filled our lungs
with the scents of flowers, fresh earth.
My '61 Austin Healy purred in overdrive.
Ninety MPH. The sun began to throw
long shadows across the highway.
The sign appeared like the Grim Reaper:
Highway 46—junction one mile.
The intersection where James Dean died,
drove his Porsche head on into a Ford.
She turned to me, face bright with life,
                    "Let's go faster."

Someday

Someday I will close my eyes
for the last time.
I will never again see
the ocean of your eyes,
the sunshine
of your smile.
I will never again hear
the music of your voice
when you whisper,
  I love you.
Yet, I will never forget you.

The Old Neighborhood

This is the alley of my childhood:
that sag of power lines, glass insulators atop
creosote soaked poles, that wooden fence
that Wilbur Johnson first painted red in '56
ignoring the protests of many neighbors.
And those two small sheds on the left
belonged to Uncle Charlie. As long as I can
remember they've needed paint. My brother
Bobby and I spent summers here. That shed
nearest the alley was our secret clubhouse.
After a rain this alley was soggy for days
with standing water. And down the way
old man Jenson battled the city constantly
about his trees and their power lines. Then,
Sara Harris moved into that big two story
at the end of the alley. She was a wisp of a girl
with red hair and emerald eyes. After that
this alley didn't seem so shabby, I didn't spend
as much time with Bobby, and for the first time
I noticed how blue the sky was.

Art raises its head where creeds relax.

Nietzsche

Greenwich Village Wedding

There is no church,
no minster,
no gathering
of family and friends.

A tangled sheet
is her wedding gown,
that faux fireplace
their witness.

He whispers
I love you and *I do,*
in the same breath.

The red velvet wallpaper
proclaims,
You may kiss the bride.

Questions

I wonder about the seagulls.
How do they know when
a minus tide will expose
the mussels that cling
to these jetty boulders?
Do they read the same
tide charts I do?
And when did they learn
to open those shells
held together as tightly
as a child's hands in prayer?

What I Should Have Said

I've come down to the sea to talk with my father.
The sky is a confusion of clouds that lie heavy
on the horizon. The sea today is a muted gray-green,
not the warm August blue ocean like that day
we waded in, cast his memory adrift on an ebb tide.
He's been gone now nearly a decade. I want to go back
to my childhood, tell him he is my hero, say things
I should have said every time I saw him. I want to go back
to those days in Seal Beach, that small white house
on Electric Avenue, my mother and me on a summer lawn
playing in the spray of a garden hose. I want to be there
when my father returns home from work, holds me
in his arms, kisses my mother and we know it will always
be this way. I want to see them one more time, be sure
they know I loved them, I'm sorry I didn't say so more often.

In Love Again

When we
married
you said
we would
grow old
together.
It's just
that I didn't
realize
it was going
to happen
in the first
two years.

Surfers, aka Shark Bait

Here's an idea. Let's dress up
like a shark's favorite food
and paddle out into the Pacific.
Be sure your wetsuit is black,
that same delicious black
as seal skin, a shark's favorite.
Then, let's kick and splash
around in the open ocean
like an injured or sick sea lion.
Be sure to dangle your feet
off the back of your board
so from deep down in the blue
abyss of the Pacific your silhouette
mimics that of, you guessed it,
a seal, a great white's delight.
But the odds are low that some
razor toothed villain of the deep
will ruin your day, possibly your life.
But then, look at the results
of the 2016 Presidential election.

Shorebird

Her small skeleton still intact
she lies on the cobbles
just above high tide line.
A few feathers still adorn her
hollow bones; tiny beak
on her long straight neck
like the head of a spear.
I don't see her legs or feet.
Scavengers have finished
with her, tiny carcass
now baking in the sun.
She is weightless
in the palm of my hand,
no smell of death,
remains delicately rigid.
I leave her where I found her
just as they left Mallory
where they found him on Everest.

Waiting

In the shadows of an old eucalyptus
I wait for the rest of my life to begin.
Above me, a crow's insistent cries
fall from a branch, like those slender
leaves that litter the sidewalk.
And in the silent seconds between
his caws and the rustling leaves
I can hear my father weep, see Mother
lying in bed, the room dark with death.

Summer Wind

I search for remnants
of our hours together
down by the sea.
I find a footprint or two
where we walked. Yet,
just as years have erased
the memory of your face,
tides have rewritten
those steps of our journey.
But the sun has not forgotten
days we worshiped it,
even as it faded into
one cloud after another.
I whisper your name
and you come back to me
on the summer wind.

The Right Light
inspired by the art of Kim Hirsch-*Lightplay*

I suppose I should ask
right up front,
is this bowl of cherries
half full or half empty?
Maybe it's not a bowl
at all. More like a slice
of the sun, planets
clustered off center
as eminent doom looms.

And the oranges:
one sliced bloodless
on the counter top
mimicking the face
of a sunflower;
the remaining two,
perfect spheres
like those obvious
breast implants
of an aging star.

Life can be anything you want
—in the right light.

Cardiac Unit
post procedure

My nurse's name is Angel,
a black woman with a generous smile
white as a new sail against a stormy sky,
her grin enhanced by a gold front tooth.
The writer Alexander McCall Smith
might call her a traditionally built woman.
I'm suddenly struck by the poetic nature
of her name. I pinch myself,
as if this will confirm—something.
Angel places a food tray in front of me.
I sample the brown meat-like substance,
instant mashed potatoes (no gravy),
green beans (no salt), coffee (decaf).
This is confirmation enough.
Even with a nurse called Angel,
                    this is not heaven.

Grandpa's Beer Stein

Peering into the shadows
of your mouth
it's as if, like a full moon,
you have swallowed the night.

In my hand, fingers conform
to your curves like a suckling child
at her mother's milk laden breast.

I lift you to my ear, wonder
if you hide something
the way a sea shell
holds the ocean prisoner.

I inhale your emptiness.
Spring comes to mind, a sea
of Green Parrot Tulips.

My tongue touches you, lightly,
like the first time with a woman.
Your taste is not familiar. Yet,
like that woman, I know I want you.

You Call My Name

Seal Beach, California, summer of '46.
I play at water's edge, fearless, wade in
too deep, feel the pull of the Pacific.
Mother, you call my name, reach for me,
your hands strong with love.

Now, I walk barefoot in the shallows.
The sea swirls cool against my skin.
Overhead, a lazy line of pelicans
drifts by in a stormy sky.

Beyond the bluff, Coast Highway
traffic hums, wrestles with the song
of the sea, that constant cascade
of waves finding their way to shore.

And today, twenty years since your death,
I thought I heard you call my name.

Tree Trimmer

He climbs to the summit of an old palm.
I'm not sure *summit* is the correct term
for the top of a tree. I know that if you
spend enough money, don't die
from lack of oxygen or severe frost bite,
you can stand on the summit of Everest.
He's equipped much like a mountain
climber. Necessary tools and rope hang
from his belt. Special foot gear allows
him to traverse treacherous tree trunks.
Naturally he carries a chainsaw. How
else would I know he's up there if not
for that high pitched, two-stroke whine?
He lops off the top, lets it flutter
to the ground. Palm fronds whirl like
helicopter blades. He slices the trunk
into chunks, lets them down by rope
and pulley. On the ground, at what
might be considered base camp, a crew
feeds everything into an extremely noisy
and nasty wood chipper. Finally, the palm
is gone, tree trimmer back on terra firma,
no hypoxia, no lose of toes or fingers
from frost bite, another successful *summit*.
Unfortunately, crows that nested in that palm,
raised their young and taught them to fly
right there in front of our eyes, will have to
search for another home. We are so efficient
at displacing our fellow earth inhabitants.

Life's Sidewalk

A March wind out of the west
dapples the sea with whitecaps.
Coastal wildflowers bow their heads
in a dance of purple and yellow.
The sky is a monochrome canvas
of slate blue. Gulls glide above
the bluff, ride invisible waves
of the cloudless morning air.
A young Egret swoops in,
begins her hunt for lizards
along the craggy bluff's edge.
In the green undergrowth
a squirrel burrows in the earth.
A lone surfer steps from the sea,
walks along the sidewalk.
Wet footprints mark his path.
They soon dry and disappear.
I've watched the footprints
of my children's childhood fade
into memories; the footprints
of my parents' lives ebb
on a tide that never returned.
Now, at seventy-five,
I check over my shoulder
to see if my footprints are fading
from life's sidewalk.

Summer Sun

Today, I came to this beach bench
to write poetry. But instead, scribble
your name over and over in my notepad
like a schoolboy with a crush.
On the sidewalk, the chaos of humanity:
a parade of children on scooters and skates;
parents push babies in strollers;
women with tan legs chase youth;
couples alone together, their iPhones
tuning each other out; skateboarders snake
their way through the weekend horde.
In the water, surfers try to finagle a wave
while along the bluff a white egret hunts
lizards, oblivious to traffic's constant murmur.
And I reach into the Sunday morning sky, catch
a handful of summer sun to take home to you.

All bad poetry springs from genuine feeling.

Oscar Wilde

Royale Road Publishing